Making Meetings Work

in a week

GRAHAM WILLCOCKS
AND STEVE MORRIS

Hodder & Stoughton

A MEMBER OF THE HODDER HEADLINE GROUP

Orders: please contact Bookpoint Ltd, 39 Milton Park, Abingdon, Oxon OX14 4TD.
Telephone: (44) 01235 400414, Fax: (44) 01235 400454. Lines are open from 9.00 -
6.00, Monday to Saturday, with a 24 hour message answering service.
Email address: orders@bookpoint.co.uk

British Library Cataloguing in Publication Data
A catalogue record for this title is available from The British Library

ISBN 0 340 772425

First published 2000
Impression number   10 9 8 7 6 5 4 3 2 1
Year   2005   2004   2003   2002   2001   2000

Copyright © 2000 Graham Willcocks and Steve Morris

All rights reserved. No part of this publication may be reproduced or
transmitted in any form or by any means, electronic or mechanical, including
photocopy, recording, or any information storage and retrieval system,
without permission in writing from the publisher or under licence from the
Copyright Licensing Agency Limited. Further details of such licences (for
reprographic reproduction) may be obtained from the Copyright Licensing
Agency Limited, of 90 Tottenham Court Road, London W1P 9HE.

Typeset by Multiplex Techniques Ltd, St Mary Cray, Kent.
Printed in Great Britain for Hodder & Stoughton Educational, a division of
Hodder Headline Plc, 338 Euston Road, London NW1 3BH by Cox & Wyman Ltd,
Reading, Berkshire.

***in** the Institute of Management*

The Institute of Management (IM) is the leading organisation for professional management. Its purpose is to promote the art and science of management in every sector and at every level, through research, education, training and development, and representation of members' views on management issues.

This series is commissioned by IM Enterprises Limited, a subsidiary of the Institute of Management, providing commercial services.

**Management House,
Cottingham Road,
Corby,
Northants NN17 1TT
Tel: 01536 204222;
Fax: 01536 201651
Website: http://www.inst-mgt.org.uk**

Registered in England no 3834492
Registered office: 2 Savoy Court, Strand,
London WC2R 0EZ

■■■■C O N T E N T S■■■■

For most of us, meetings take up an enormous amount of time. Some people seem to spend all their lives, dashing out of one meeting to get to the next one. As someone who hates meetings said: 'When do they ever get the chance to do any work?'

Sometimes meetings are worthwhile, but all too often they achieve little, and waste the time you could be spending on something more productive. The difference between the effective meetings and the rest has nothing to do with the topic, the timing or the location. It all depends on the person setting it up and running it. Some people do it really well, while others...

This week we're going to look at that difference, and set out the steps to make your meetings work well:

Sunday	Know which meetings to hold and which to ditch
Monday	Prepare, prepare and prepare again
Tuesday	Taking time with paper work
Wednesday	Effective chairing
Thursday	Dealing with difficult people and problems
Friday	The follow-up
Saturday	Special meetings

The good, the bad and the ones to stop holding

Nearly everyone complains about meetings; there are probably too many and there are certainly too many that don't work. The problem is that they're an everyday part of life and we're used to putting up with them.

Some meetings are very useful and well run, but there are too many that are far less productive than they could and should be – and all too often they're a downright waste of time. But, usually, we don't stand back and look at what we could do to get more from our meetings. We're so used to spending time in meetings that don't work, that we do nothing about it except complain afterwards. If meetings are to be effective, this has to change, and we need to start with an overview of some of the crucial background issues. So today we'll look at:

- What makes a good meeting and why so many fail to make the grade
- The cost of a meeting
- How to spot which meetings we need and which we don't
- Taking a fresh view of tired and routine meetings.

Then, during the rest of the week, we will look in more detail at how to get the best out of the meetings we do need.

What makes an effective meeting?

Think about a meeting you've been to recently that someone else arranged and which was particularly effective. Make a few notes about why you think it was effective – what were the characteristics of this meeting that made it a success? Then do the opposite. Think of a recent meeting that someone else arranged, that you left feeling especially despondent, frustrated, angry or generally negative. What was it about this meeting that made it such a dreadful failure?

If a group of us compared notes, the points we would include would be pretty similar – although we might list them in a different order. The same factors apply to all meetings, whether they're positive and effective, or negative and a total waste of time. What makes the difference is that the factors are there for a good meeting, while they're missing at a bad one.

We thought we would draw up a humorous checklist for meetings, listing some of the most irritating and negative points we could think of. The sad thing is, we found it wasn't funny at all, because it bears an uncanny resemblance to real life. What do you think?

The devil's guide to meetings
Here are twenty keypoints to having the worst meetings ever.

1 Schedule a meeting for as imminent a time as possible.

2 Do absolutely no preparation; never read anything in advance.

3   Decide that you'll wing it or busk it… improvise at the meeting.

4   Turn up early for the meeting and expect to start it straightaway.

5   Turn up late and make everyone stand up as you struggle to a seat.

6   Arrive straight after an agenda item where your input is vital, so everyone has to go through it again.

7   Forget to bring the agenda and all other papers (or better still, bring the wrong papers with you).

8   Hog the coffee, scoff all the biscuits and smack your lips loudly.

9   Rustle papers and tap your pen loudly during the meeting.

10 Slump in your chair, arms folded and legs apart, occasionally leaning back to sigh loudly as you look out of the window.

11 Make comments to your neighbour in an audible stage whisper, and start you own mini-meeting during someone else's discussion.

12 Interrupt the meeting regularly and ask pointless questions.

13 Introduce points that weren't on the agenda and no one has had time to prepare for.

14 Argue your point angrily, as if you're the only one with a brain.

15 Take offence at every possible opportunity… you're still the only one with a brain.

16 Answer in monosyllables when asked for your opinion.

17 Leave the meeting (loudly) to visit the loo or have a cigarette as often as possible.

18 Raise lots of niggling queries at the end, to drag the meeting out.

19 Use the meeting as a forum for gossip.

20 Make sure your mobile phone and alarm watch are turned on with charged batteries (seasoned meeting devils arrange for phone calls at critical times and set their alarm to beep every half hour).

It's a safe bet that even if you've never sinned, you know several people who between them do all these things regularly. And the bottom line is that it can't be funny because it's real. Seeing even a couple of these things leaves you frustrated and annoyed at having to waste time on such a bad experience. We need to turn all these things round and produce effective and productive meetings.

The recipe for a good meeting

1   Everyone understands the meeting's aims and objectives.

2   People know why they're there, and they come prepared.

3   The right people are there (and the wrong ones aren't).

4   What was agreed at the last meeting (if there was one) is clear in the minutes or action notes.

5   The agenda spells out what will happen at the meeting. Its structure reflects the priorities and the meeting runs to the agenda.

6   Discussion is relevant, useful and contained to the point.

7   Talkative people aren't allowed to hog it, so the quieter ones with a real contribution to make get the chance to make it.

8   It lasts as long as necessary and no longer.

9   Decisions are taken and actions are planned to take things forward.

10   The meeting's objectives are reached.

11   Everyone leaves knowing what has been agreed, so they can take the action they're committed to.

The acid test for a successful meeting is whether the people who were at the meeting can explain what happened and what was achieved afterwards.

You'll know from your own experience that meetings that lack two, three or more of these key characteristics are the ones you find frustrating. But it's important to remember that we live in the real world and it's rare to find them all covered at the same meeting. The more of the positive characteristics a meeting has, though, the more effective it is.

So what do you do about it, now you have clarified the characteristics of an effective meeting? The answer is that it depends on whether you're in other people's meetings or at ones you set up and run yourself. It's harder to influence the shape of other people's meetings, but there are some things you can do and we will look at these throughout the week.

Where you can have most impact is on your own meetings, because the common factor that links the characteristics of a good meeting is that someone has to plan it and make it happen. It doesn't occur accidentally and it's the person running the meeting who has to prepare the ground, manage the business effectively and efficiently, keep the discussion on track and give regular clear summaries about what has been agreed and who does what, by when.

We will look at these issues throughout the week, especially on Wednesday and Thursday, when we focus on the chair of the meeting.

Why good meetings matter

Organisations don't grind to a halt because they have unproductive meetings. Things still seem to get done, so why are we so worried?

There are several reasons for making meetings work. They include:

- The negative effect that ineffective meetings have on morale, motivation and productivity
- The lost time that could be spent taking things forward: if you weren't shut in a room for three hours think of what else you achieve – and multiply that by the number of people there
- Their expense and there has to be a pay-back; it's easy to work out the cost of a meeting – just assess the various salaries and break them down to the time the meeting takes.

Let's take a simple example, a meeting lasting three hours, involving eight people, and use that to explore the three issues in the above list.

First, think about the effect if half the people come out of the meeting switched off. Four otherwise productive individuals slump wearily in their chairs and go over the meeting in their minds afterwards, losing concentration and patience, and not working at their best for some time.

Then there's the time. Eight people for three hours is three days' work, in raw terms. It's actually much more than that as their separate skills, expertise and talents are all lost to the organisation for the time the meeting lasts. Then there's the extra time that other people spend covering for them, answering the phone, responding to queries, taking messages and generally holding the fort instead of getting on with their own job.

Finally there's the cost, which we're working out very conservatively, here. If the average salary of the eight people is £26,000, we can say that they each get £500 a week, or £100 a day. Say the meeting lasts 30% of a day, that's £30 per individual. Multiply that by eight, add the 15% or so for on-costs (National Insurance, employment costs and so on) and it's about £280 for the meeting. And that doesn't include the time spent preparing for the meeting or getting there and back. We could put the cost up to £350.

So the questions that have to be asked are:

- Does this meeting produce enough real benefit to justify losing three days of other productive work, at a cost of £350?

> • Does the meeting add value, or does it waste time and cause us to lose momentum, when people get frustrated, bored and negative?

If the answers aren't completely positive it really is time either to scrap the meeting or to take a long hard look at how to make it work better.

Breaking bad habits

Before moving on to look at how to make meetings work, let's start by reviewing whether the meeting is necessary at all. It's a bad habit to go along to a meeting just because it's in the diary, so think about breaking the habit.

Does the 'Thursday morning meeting' ring a bell (it could be any day). The point is that this meeting is known by when it happens, not what it's for, and that's the clue. The fact that 'it's Thursday' is not a good enough reason to hold a meeting.

Picture the scene. It's Thursday morning so it's time for the weekly meeting that started years ago as a way of 'communicating better within the team'. You know it's going to last two hours because it always does, however much there is to talk about. And it always starts late. Each week the same two people turn up fifteen minutes after the start and apologise. For the benefit of the late-comers the person running the meeting goes over the same ground they've just covered, so the meeting starts again.

There's no real discussion because everyone wants to get on with something else, so they're frightened to start a debate about anything important. Instead it's the usual ritual of giving out information that could have been written down and sent round as a note. It grinds its way through the morning until everyone escapes with a huge sigh of relief, heading for a cup of coffee and a twenty minute rest to talk about what a dreadful meeting it was and how they're now behind with everything else.

The solution

The solution to this sort of petrified meeting is actually quite simple. At the end of one meeting tell everyone that the only item for discussion next time is the meeting itself. Say you're going to ask three questions:

1 What is the purpose of the meeting?
2 How well does it achieve that purpose?
3 What are we going to do to improve it?

Then discuss it at the next meeting with a completely open mind, taking careful note of the points that come out and agreeing a way forward. Don't be frightened to make radical changes, like cutting it to once a fortnight or down to an hour, and/or having agenda items that individuals have to introduce. You know the costs involved, so you can easily work out the savings that come from halving the time spent.

It's quite straightforward to turn this sort of meeting from a virtual waste of time into a positive and active experience. It's simply a question of breaking out of the lazy habit of using it as a forum for passing round standard information.

Over time, a meeting like this can be the fixed focal point for people to communicate with each other. The result can be information starvation, with information failing to pass round the team during the week as everyone saves it all up for 'the Thursday meeting'. Breaking out solves the starvation problem and it's far more productive to use the time for constructive team activity, like identifying potential quality improvements and planning their implementation.

And don't write off the most radical option, scrapping it altogether, if the benefits of the meeting are clearly outweighed by the costs.

Many people have regular meetings outside work, at a sports club or social group. So if this applies to you, think about breaking the cycle of these meetings, as well.

The solution for your meetings
When you run meetings you want other people to value them, make a full contribution and get something out of them. To make sure you continue getting it right, take stock occasionally and check that the timetable for meetings and the way they run is appropriate. Just because it was the right arrangement three years ago doesn't mean it's still right, so ask yourself, and the other people at the meeting, five simple questions:

- What is the current purpose of these meetings?
- Has the purpose changed since they started?
- Is the current timetable of meetings appropriate for what we do?
- Do we need to meet less or more frequently, or as we do now?
- How else can we improve our meetings?

The solution for other people's meetings
With other people's meetings you need to consider whether it's worth going at all. There are two questions to consider and they come from opposite ends of the equation:

1 If I go, can I make a contribution that justifies my being there?
2 Is this the best use of my time?

The first issue is about whether the meeting will miss you if you're not there. The second is about your own priorities.

On rare occasions you might find that the answer is 'no' to both and then the answer is clear. You're not needed and you have better things to do.

But it's rarely that clear-cut, and the balance between the two issues might pull you in one direction rather than the other. It's more likely that you can find better things to do, but your contribution really does make an important difference. Deciding where the balance lies is an individual matter for you. (However, if you haven't got anything else you could do at work, I'd keep quiet about it and I wouldn't bother reading on.)

Summary

Today we've looked at:

- The characteristics of an effective meeting
- Why it's important that meetings are effective (and cost-effective)
- Reviewing and revitalising routine meetings
- Whether you need to break out of the cycle of routine.

Tomorrow we start to look at preparing for meetings, whether they're yours or someone else's.

Don't fail to prepare

There's an old saying, that failing to prepare is the same as preparing to fail. This applies whether it's your meeting or someone else's.

Meetings you run

Think about the way your normal meetings work...
and you can be honest because you don't have to share your thoughts with anyone else.

Do they ever frequently or always:

- Start late as people drift in, so you stop to welcome them and then recap on what's already gone, for their benefit
- Encourage people not to bother talking to each other during the week, as they think 'I'll wait until I see them at the meeting'
- Consist entirely of items you've put on the agenda, with other people raising important matters at the last minute under AOB
- Spend too much time on trivial matters, while important issues get deferred or cut short because there's no time left
- Get hi-jacked by one or two forceful people who raise off-the-cuff items and steal the time you planned to spend on other matters
- Ramble on through irrelevant topics that should be dealt with outside the meeting.

If you can honestly say that none of these happen in your meetings, you're doing very well already. But they are common problems and most of us have suffered from one or more of them, from time to time. What they have in common is that proper preparation can dramatically reduce them all.

Three stages of preparation

There are three levels of preparation for the meetings you run. One is the detailed work you do once you know what's on the agenda, and another is arranging the practical details for the meeting. We will look at those shortly, but the first stage is about the overall meeting process, rather than the content of, or arrangements for, any single meeting. This stage is particularly powerful as a way of removing the problems we looked at above.

Stage 1: Setting guidelines

This stage gives you the freedom to decide how to make your meetings effective through a set of clear guidelines that you construct and issue to everyone else. You may want to consult other people about them but the final decision is yours. So if you want to, you can issue them without negotiation, based purely on your own professional judgement. The only constraint is that you must be certain they will meet your own needs and deliver the sort of effective meetings you want. The process for setting guidelines for meetings is that you:

* Decide how you want to organise your meetings
* Consult anyone whose views you value and want to hear
* Write down the guidelines
* Send them out, making it clear that this is how things will be.

They then become the standard framework for every meeting. Some people will complain, because they always do when something changes. But the chances are that if you consulted the people who make sound contributions to your meetings, the complainers will be the people whose behaviour you want to change...the ones who turn up late, don't prepare, raise issues off-the-cuff or wait until 'any other business' to bring up important issues that deserve a full airing in the main meeting.

Some sample guidelines
These are one manager's guidelines for meeting arrangements. Yours may be different but this example shows you one approach, as a starter for drawing up your own.

1   The attendance list is fixed. People not on the list, including substitutes, only attend if it is cleared with me in advance.

2   Agenda items go to Pat by noon, five working days before the meeting. This is a strict deadline. If no substantial items are received you will be notified that day that the meeting is cancelled.

3   If you put forward an agenda item you must indicate when you submit it, whether it is for (a) information, (b) discussion or (c) decision, and how long you estimate it will take on the agenda.

4   The general rule is that supporting papers, reports, etc. accompany the notification, five days ahead. If you plan to table papers at the meeting you should discuss it with me when you submit the agenda item.

5   At the meeting you introduce and lead any item you put on the agenda.

6   Meetings start promptly and end on time. We do not go over matters we have already covered for the benefit of people who turn up late.

7   If you need to leave before the end you must make this clear – in any event before the meeting starts and, if you are leading an agenda item, at the time you notify it (five days ahead).

8   The first agenda item is to construct Any Other
     Business. The general rule is that AOB is for emergency
     or very short information items and is not a substitute
     for significant matters that should be on the main
     agenda. The only points allowed under AOB at the end
     of the meeting are those that have been raised and
     agreed at the start.

9   The second agenda item is to check progress of action
     points (who does what, by when) from the last
     meeting, not covered elsewhere on the agenda.

The benefits of guidelines

The example above has some powerful benefits, and reflects
a lot of good practice. For instance, these guidelines:

- Send out a consistent message about what will
  happen, so there's no confusion or misunderstanding
- Focus the minds of people who don't take the
  meeting seriously, because they show themselves
  up if they come late or don't prepare
- Brings the standard up to that of the people who
  have always prepared, so that best practice is more
  widespread
- Avoid unnecessary meetings, if there's nothing
  worth meeting for
- Help shape the agenda (which we look at in more
  detail tomorrow)
- Balance the shape of the meeting, with important
  issues discussed during the main meeting and AOB
  as a minor addition

> • Respect the people who turn up on time, so they don't have to sit through a repeat of what they've already covered for the benefit of those who don't have the manners to arrive promptly.

Not only do techniques like these improve the way the meeting runs, they spread the ownership of the meeting away from just you, to a wider responsibility among everyone who attends. Now they all have a stake in it and that increases the effort other people put into getting it right.

The manager who devised these guidelines had a few initial difficulties, but sticking to the rules meant that everyone had to come round to best practice, and soon adopted the guidelines for themselves.

'*The very first meeting after I'd issued the guidelines was cancelled. Nobody gave us any agenda items, so I called it off.*

There was minor uproar, but I simply pointed to the guidelines and told them I wasn't going to presume that I knew better than them. They'd told me (by saying nothing) that they didn't need that meeting, so I was just going along with them because they were grown-ups. It wasn't for me to override their decisions not to meet, but if they did want the meeting they had to take responsibility for their own actions (and inaction).

Then, when we had a meeting, the same people came in late. We didn't go over old ground and they looked quite lost. But the people who were there on time really appreciated it, because it didn't waste their time and they had made the effort.

The AOB guideline worked really well. The first time we worked to it I refused to take any of the four items people raised because they were important enough to go on the main agenda. Now everyone accepts that the guidelines are how we do business, and our meetings are much more productive.'

Stage 2: practical details

The second stage of preparing for your own meetings is organising the physical details – lack of attention to the simple things can really foul up a meeting. You need to:

- Book the room, or check it's available
- Arrange for any refreshments
- Book any equipment you need (OHP, flip chart, pencils, pads, etc.)

- Confirm the meeting is on, by reviewing the agenda items submitted
- Construct and send out a reminder of the meeting, along with the Agenda and copies of any supporting materials.

On the day of the meeting, get there early (or delegate someone else to do so) and check the fine points of detail such as whether the table and chairs are in the right place, that the previous people left the room tidy, and that the equipment and other materials have arrived. It might sound trivial, but there's nothing worse than arriving on time and having to spend ten minutes moving furniture, or chasing up the coffee. It's even worse to find the equipment isn't there and you've let down someone who told you in plenty of time that they wanted to show a video clip as part of their item, or needed an OHP to show some figures.

Home or away

Setting up and confirming the physical arrangements shouldn't be too problematic if you are using a room you know well, or have been in for meetings before. But it can be very different if you are holding a meeting away from your home ground, maybe in a conference centre or at an hotel.

There are some simple guidelines to follow if you are having an away meeting. Some of them might sound trivial, but it's important to remember that it's the tiny things that make the difference. For instance, if you don't drink coffee and that's all that's provided, your attention is diverted from the business in hand; you feel aggrieved that you have been neglected, and either you or someone else spends time chasing up to bring you something extra. So, pay attention to the following:

- Always go in person and check everything with the people providing the room and the facilities.
- Try and take someone else along with you, especially if it's a large meeting in a large space. Another pair of eyes might spot something you miss. Also, you can try out the acoustics and feel how different seating arrangements work.
- If you have a choice of rooms, pick one that's the right size. You would naturally avoid one that's clearly too small, knowing that it gets hot and uncomfortable. In cramped conditions an individual's 'personal space' is almost certain to be threatened, and people find it difficult to move round the room to make a presentation, or even take a comfort break. But having a room that's much too big can be just as bad, because people can feel exposed and inhibited if the meeting is huddled round a table in one corner of a huge ballroom.

- Confirm the price, and what you get for the money. For instance, it's quite common for a video player to cost an extra £50 or so.
- Check what's happening immediately before and after you need the room – is there a danger you'll have to wait for someone else to clear out, or are you going to be chased out yourselves when another group wants to get in.
- If you're using any of the host's technology, see it while it is working and get someone to show you how to use it. If you don't, it won't start when you want it to or you will be flapping around trying to find out how the projector switches on.
- If you're taking your own equipment, find out where the power points are. Take an extension lead if necessary.
- If you want a flip chart, make sure there are serviceable marker pens on hand.
- Be very specific about the seating arrangements. Don't assume that your understanding of a 'boardroom' layout is necessarily the same as theirs; show them what you expect by moving furniture around.
- Specify the fine details of the catering such as when you want refreshments, whether you want tea and/or coffee, and water on the tables. If it's an all-day affair, find out about the lunch arrangements and remember to cater for vegetarians and other special diets.
- Familiarise yourself with the other domestic arrangements – where the toilets are, what the fire alarm sounds like and what the fire drill is.

- When you get back to the office send a fax to confirm everything you've agreed, including a diagram of the seating arrangements.

Stage 3: managing the meeting

This stage has a lot in common with the preparation you need for someone else's meeting. It's about the detailed content of the meeting and, if it's your meeting, you have to think about both the agenda items and the way you plan to manage the meeting. You need to:

- Look at the minutes/action notes from the last meeting, to remind yourself how things were left and what was to be done between then and now
- Read the agenda and anticipate what might happen
- Run through the meeting in your mind, to make sure it all fits together and is achievable in the time allowed
- Study any background papers, so you're ready for the discussion
- Anticipate any problems (like a potential clash between two people you know have opposing views on a topic) and plan how to handle it
- Identify any contribution you want to make on a topic that's coming up (or whether you have nothing to say unless something crops up)
- Prepare to present any agenda items that you have raised.

How the meeting thinks and takes decisions
One point to consider is the way you want the meeting to

think about a particular item. The choice is between convergent thinking or divergent thinking:

- Divergent thinking opens up options and enhances creativity, by asking people to look for alternatives, instead of aiming for one right answer (on Saturday there's more information on meetings that are specifically set up to achieve this)
- Convergent thinking narrows down options and searches for the right answer, in the same way that most try and work out calculations, or do those logic problems.

Many items need both approaches, in sequence, and you need to think about how you want your colleagues to approach a discussion, so you can make it clear what's expected of them, and manage the process effectively. For instance, imagine you work in an NHS Trust which has two hospitals a mile apart. Hospital A sends blood samples to B's laboratory by taxi, and it's time to renew the contract and select from a range of tenders. But before renewing the contract you want to check on all the other possible options, just in case there's an easier, quicker and/or faster way. Looking for these alternatives involves divergent thinking, because it's about opening up the options rather than narrowing them down.

Your role is to encourage people to think freely, use their imagination and creativity, and open up the options as widely as they can. If you don't help the meeting take a creative approach, the possibility is that no one will think of any alternatives. But if you help them to open their minds, you could end up with a whole range of options, from the current taxi contract to a runner, and from someone on a moped to carrier pigeons.

Once you have the full range of options listed it's time to evaluate them against criteria, using a logical and systematic approach. That's convergent thinking – looking for the right answer based on evidence, statistics and clear performance criteria. At this point you need to stop people from taking a creative approach. Now is the time for analysis and attention to detail. The point of working out which style of discussion you want is that it helps the people at your meeting to make a more relevant and constructive contribution, if you, and they, are clear about the way this item is going to be tackled.

That's about it for your own meetings. But you need to prepare for other people's meetings, too.

Other people's meetings

Yesterday we looked at breaking out, including breaking out of other people's meetings. Reviewing the importance and relevance of each meeting means you can be pretty sure that the ones you're going to are worth your time.

If you are going to other people's meetings, follow your own best practice principles, even if the person running the meeting hasn't sent out guidelines. Put yourself in the shoes of someone coming to one of your own meetings and behave as well as you would like them to, so you will:

• Notify the meeting organiser well in advance if you want to raise an agenda item, and send them any supporting papers

- Let them know as soon as you do if you can't make it, feel a substitute could attend for you, or may have to leave before the end of the meeting
- Read the minutes/action notes carefully, so you know what happened last time, and know that you haven't forgotten to do something you agreed to
- Find the agenda items that are relevant to you, or where you want to make a contribution, so you can prepare properly; do this to avoid surprises and, if there's a chance you may disagree with someone else, the possibility that they could wrong-foot you because they have done their homework
- If you're not sure what an item means, ring up and ask in advance
- Make sure you turn up on time – or send apologies in advance.

Summary

The main point about what we've looked at today is that sound preparation is crucial – especially when it's for your own meeting, but also when it's for someone else's. Setting out some guidelines gives everyone the same clear picture of how your meetings will operate, and it helps raise the standard across the board. Then, as long as you've covered the physical details and taken an advance look at what each meeting is likely to throw up, you've started to take control.

Tomorrow we look in more detail at the paperwork for meetings and develop the issues we've started to look at today: on minutes that help ensure the right action is taken, and agendas that act as a plan for the meeting.

Making the paper work

The notes of the last meeting and the agenda for this one are a crucial part of the preparation we looked at yesterday. Today we expand this and link the minutes and the agenda to the actual running of the meeting.

Minutes of the last meeting

If a meeting is one of a series or it's a regular event, the record of what happened at the last meeting is a vital starting point for the next one. Whether they're called minutes, action notes or simply notes of the meeting, they share the need for accuracy and clarity, but there are also some fundamental differences. You do need to look at the options and decide which format you want to use.

Minutes
Minutes tend to be a full narrative outline of the meeting, detailing who said what, and what happened, and in which order. That might be the way you want to play it, but in most circumstances you can achieve a tighter result with a summary of the key points and a clear list of what was agreed. The advantage of a full set of minutes is that there's a record of everything to look back at, in case there's a detailed query about who said what. But in most cases the disadvantages outweigh the benefits, because minutes:

- take a lot of time to produce
- use several trees to produce the amount of paper they generate

- are complex and difficult to write, which is why most meetings with full minutes have a clerk who does little else but take notes during the meeting
- take a fair time to read and find your way through.

However, there are some meetings which need this level of recording, for example, when opposing factions put forward conflicting ideas and principles at a local council debate, or groups of representatives from various bodies meet to spend large amounts of other people's money.

Action notes
In most work and social meetings action notes are a better bet and add more value than minutes. Action notes highlight future action rather than past debate, so they're often more appropriate and effective for work meetings than a full 'Hansard' version of the discussion.

Action notes don't cover all the narrative detail of who said what and when, but they accurately record what was decided, and they're a crystal clear list of who is doing what. If they're not, you get confusion, blame and recrimination – something you'll recognise if you've ever been at a meeting and discovered that your perception of what was agreed last time is different from other's people's recollections.

There are two rules about action notes:

> 1 Make sure they're absolutely clear about who is committed to doing what, by when.
> 2 Make sure you always stick to rule 1.

We will look at writing up formats for action notes on Friday when we explore how to follow up the meeting.

It's worth taking a few moments at the beginning of the meeting, so everyone can discuss whether minutes or action notes are the better option. It gives them the chance to contribute to the process and increases their ownership of what is agreed. Put forward the options and discuss which one fits the bill.

The agenda for the next meeting

The guidelines we looked at yesterday, where you require people to identify agenda items in advance and produce reports or supporting papers at the same time, give you the chance to plan, prepare and distribute the agenda in good time. Not just any agenda, but an effective one. After all, the agenda is an important working document, more important than you might imagine from the quality of some that we've seen.

The purpose of the agenda

For many people the agenda is just the information about where and when the meeting is, and which issues are going to be looked at. That's certainly a key function, but it has another potential use as well. An agenda can serve as an extremely powerful planning tool, to outline:

- How different topics are to be handled
- Who is raising them and why
- Whether there's any special preparation needed
- How long each item is likely to take.

An agenda that's put together in this way gives everyone a clearer picture of the meeting they're going to. It sets the objectives, clarifies the priorities, explains who is doing what and, at the very least, gives a good estimate of the time it will take.

All this simply reinforces the importance of the preparation stage, because you can't take this constructive line without the guidelines we looked at yesterday.

Standard agenda items

All agendas must say what the meeting is, where it is and when. Most agendas then have a few regular items:

- Apologies for absence – who isn't here and why
- Minutes or notes from the last meeting – are they a correct record
- Matters arising – anything that was covered at the last meeting that needs an update, because the same topic isn't on the agenda as a main item this time.

Drop these if you can, and in most cases it's quite easy to do so. With accurate action notes you should be able to do away with the bits about minutes, and getting rid of the formal and archaic 'Apologies for absence' makes the meeting feel more vibrant and relevant. You can always just say who isn't there, without a nineteenth-century agenda item.

Any other business

We mentioned AOB yesterday. It is a fairly standard item on nearly all agendas, but it benefits from some very critical thought for two reasons.

The first is the possibility that an important point, that really merits its own slot on the agenda, can be left until AOB. It happens far too often and it's the result of either laziness or poor preparation. The result is that a vital piece of information or a problem is launched on an unsuspecting group in a part of the agenda that's not designed to take major items. If an urgent decision is needed it's likely to be rushed and badly thought through, and important information gets overlooked as people start packing their bags and thinking about their next appointment.

The second reason is that an AOB is the place where a lot of absolute trivia comes up, stuff that nobody is interested in or wants to spend time on. When this happens, it devalues the rest of the meeting and the whole event slides to an end, with people muttering and grumbling as they stop paying any attention and begin to moan.

There are basically two options on AOB (leaving it as it is, at the end of the agenda, is not an option!). The options are:

1 Take it off the agenda completely, arguing that all important business should be notified in advance, and anything urgent should be dealt with properly in other ways but not in a meeting.

2 Control it by asking at the start of the meeting whether anyone wants to raise an AOB item at the end. That way you can get them to give you a ten-second summary, and decide whether it merits a place.

Option 1 is the ideal. We strongly recommend that you choose it if it's at all possible. But if it's simply too radical then move on to option 2. Option 2 does two things. It means you can plan what is coming up later and allow a reasonable amount of time. It also puts up a barrier to trivial items or points that are too important to be left to AOB. It focuses people's minds when they know they have to justify an item and it solves a lot of the problems you had before.

Substantial items

Some agendas just list the topics: next year's budget, overtime arrangements, publicity. But when people see a list like this, they start putting their own interpretation on things. One individual assumes that next year's budget is going to be the boss explaining how the new budget looks; someone else thinks it must be about cuts; a third reason assumes it's going to be a request for ideas. So simply saying 'next year's budget' is at best of little use, and at worst completely confusing. To avoid this assumption trap, there are a few steps you can take, to clarify each item and to help you use the agenda as a planning tool for an effective and efficient meeting.

Planning effective agendas

The starting point is that same one again... prepare
properly. Either use guidelines or find out what you need
to know to complete the points on this checklist. The key to
a sound agenda is to give all the basic information when
you list each item – who is raising it, what preparation is
needed (e.g., read the background papers), how long it
should take and why it's there.

Planning the sequence
It is important to say who is essential to an item so there's
no doubt about whether an individual needs to be there.
You also need to structure the items so anything that
doesn't involve everyone comes at the end; that way the
people who aren't needed don't have to sit through an
irrelevant session.

Justify each item
Make sure you state clearly why each item is there. It's
generally for one of three reasons:

• To get a decision,
• Share information or discuss something
• Find a solution to a problem or reach a common point
  of view.

Stating why an item is up for discussion actually gives you
an objective – you know the outcome you want to achieve.
If you cover the 'who', 'how long' and 'why', and mention
any preparation needed, you'll have an agenda that gives
you control, helps you plan and gives everyone the
information they need to make a positive contribution.

An agenda checklist

- Don't forget the basics – when and where the meeting is
- Only if you must have them, list the standard items (apologies, minutes, matters arising, AOB)
- For all substantial items state:
  - Who is introducing them
  - What preparation other people should do (including whether there are papers attached, or to be tabled)
  - How long you expect them to take (a realistic estimate plus five or ten minutes)
  - Whether they're for information, decision or discussion
  - Who must be there

The final agenda could look something like this.

Sports day planning meeting
9.20 a.m., 1 July, Room 717

Apologies for absence, notes of the last meeting, matters arising, and screen items for AOB. (*Only if you really must have these!*)

Finances

Who: JJK
Preparation: Please read the attached summary of 1999 accounts.
How long: 20 minutes
Objective: To decide: We have the same budget as last year, + 3% for inflation. Do we use it on the same activities, or cut some and/or add new ones?
Needed: Everyone

Car parking

Who: L McK
How long: 15 minutes
Objective: To discuss: This year we do not have approval to use the main car park. We can have car park 5 instead and that should be enough.
Does anyone foresee any problems?
Needed: Everyone

Prize presentation

Who: GT
How long: 5 minutes
Objective: To discuss: The chairman can't come. We need to ask our departmental director, who is available.
Needed: LMcK, GT, and PMT.

It takes a little bit more time to produce an agenda like this one, but it's an investment that saves a lot of wasted effort during the meeting itself. Everyone coming to the meeting knows what they have to prepare for, exactly what they are discussing and to what purpose. The acid test is whether you'd be happy to go to a meeting knowing everything that this agenda tells you, or whether you'd rather be kept in the dark and have the events unfold during the meeting, as a surprise.

Summary

Paperwork matters. It helps you clarify what happened at the last meeting, and make sensible plans for the next one. You cannot do it without the right amount of preparation, but once you've got into the habit of producing the right quality of notes and agendas, it becomes an easy habit and it makes a disproportionate difference. You'll find that the paperwork helps with tomorrow's topic too, when we look at what makes an effective chairperson in a meeting.

Take the chair

Yesterday we looked at how the paperwork helps structure the meeting and set out a sensible way for it to run. But the meeting itself is a group of human beings sitting around talking, so there's a good chance it could veer off and head in a quite different direction unless the chairperson ('chair') holds it together effectively. Poor chairing is the most frequent cause of ineffective meetings, so today we concentrate on what makes a good chair. We will help you to develop strategies to run your meetings, and play a constructive part in other people's.

The chairperson's role

A meeting is a process and the chair is there to manage the process. Excellent chairs manage things quietly and subtly, without trying to show everyone that they're in charge all the time. That comes from confidence, and a clear understanding of what the role's about. The essential point is to ensure that the meeting meets its objectives. To achieve this the chair has to:

- Stay 'above' the meeting and watch how the process is unfolding
- Maintain neutrality and an open mind
- Help everyone make their contribution effectively and efficiently
- Keep the atmosphere constructive and positive
- Keep the meeting on track and stop it drifting
- Encourage people to behave properly, in a mature way and with respect for their colleagues and the meeting

> • Summarise and reflect back on progress to help everyone else keep their bearings.

Not everyone is naturally good at this. Look at this list and think of people who you know are skilled at the role – and, then think of some you know who aren't. Try and work out why the good ones are good, and the bad ones are bad. Then look at yourself critically and decide where your own strengths and weaknesses lie.

Who is in the chair?
The chair is often the most senior person at the meeting or the individual who set it up in the first place. But sometimes there's a 'rotating chair', where everyone gets a turn at chairing. In a meeting between different organisations, there is sometimes a political decision to give each organisation their time, but when it's for a work or a social meeting a rotating chair is often a cop-out.

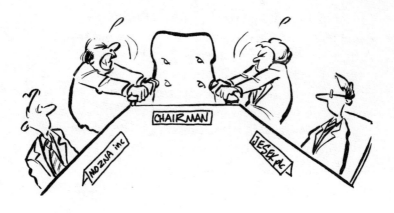

The idea of letting everyone take a turn at chairing the meeting sounds wonderfully democratic and inclusive. But the chair has a special role to play and needs to watch the process as it unfolds – like the conductor of an orchestra who keeps things together and makes sure all the various parts are played at the right level.

The danger in letting everyone take a turn is that sometimes the person whose turn it is does not have the skills needed to manage the process. They have another contribution to make, and they could be keen to get involved in the detail. So if the personality of this week's chair means they're determined to keep contributing to every item, they end up hogging the detailed discussion, and losing their grip on managing the overall process of the meeting.

Another problem with rotating the chair is that some people really hate doing it. If they know they are going to have to take it on, they worry and fret about it as the meeting gets ever closer. It can destroy and dilute their enthusiasm for the meeting and their commitment to it, and it prevents them playing a constructive role that they're comfortable with.

If you don't feel confident as a chair, look back at the cheklist on p44 and identify the things that you need to work on. Ask someone whom you respect as a chair for advice, to back up the tips you're getting here. If you're ready for a really radical alternative, give the job to someone else who's naturally good at it. It makes best use of their skills and it leaves you free to make your contribution in a different way.

Managing the chair

There's a common structure to most meetings, so we'll follow it through from start to finish. Doing the things we cover here makes a tremendous difference to the effectiveness of your meetings; most of the issues are ones that you looked at as characteristics of good meetings on Sunday.

Setting the scene
If you're the chair, your role at the start of the meeting is to:

- Get everyone quiet and welcome them to the meeting
- Check that everyone received the agenda and has the notes from last time
- Confirm the agenda and remind people what's on it – they had it some time ago so it pays to get everyone focused on it

- If there's anything unusual, such as an outsider joining you for one item, confirm what it says on the agenda and say who they are, why they're coming and what for
- Sort out any emergency items for AOB (if you went for Option 1, yesterday) and make sure the agenda can still cope with the amount on it. If there's a real emergency you have to discuss, you can either extend the meeting or cut one of the other items; it's a choice you have to make in the light of the actual circumstances at the time and it's best made by the whole meeting, sharing ownership.

The main agenda items

When you get to the main agenda items, you've already sorted out what happens next in your preparation and on the agenda. You know who's introducing the item and what the objective is, so it's simply a question of reminding everyone to ensure there's a common perception. The real chairing skills come into play once the item starts. If things are running smoothly there's no point in jumping in, but there are several occasions when you might need to intervene. Here are some of the most common which you'll probably recognise.

1   Keep the discussion on track

If you don't control the direction and focus of the discussion, someone will hi-jack the item and take it down a blind alley. It's important to take action as soon as you see that the conversation is drifting away from your objective. If you do need to stop a discussion and bring it back on track, try to soften the blow with a comment like:

'That's interesting, but we need to concentrate on this point. Perhaps we can look at that side of it another time.'

Depending on the people in the meeting, you might need to do this fairly often. And it can be quite difficult if you're the sort of individual who's uncomfortable having to put someone in their place. That's why it helps to soften the blow, because you avoid antagonising the person who led the discussion away. You feel OK about doing it, they don't feel bad because you've been tactful, and the rest of the participants will be delighted that they have a chair who makes sure things stay on course!

2 Control interruptions

It's quite common for the person who's making a point to be interrupted. Try to limit interruptions because they stop the flow of the meeting and almost certainly lead to a side-track. Part of the chair's role is to protect the person speaking and you have to be on your toes. If you don't deal with an interruption there and then, it's too late, you'll lose control. All that's needed is a quick: *'Hang on a minute, John. Lucy's still speaking. I'll come back to you on that point in a minute. OK? Thanks. Lucy, carry on.'*

Use some body language to reinforce the point and you'll be home and dry. Just add some weight to your point by leaning forward slightly, and holding your hand out, palm down.

3 Read the body language

People say a lot without opening their mouths. The chair has to draw contributions from people who have a point of view or a question but find difficulty expressing it without help. Watch for signs that someone:

- Is holding back because they're shy or reserved – little signals like a furrowed brow or a quizzical look
- Is trying to say something, but gets beaten to it because other people are more aggressive, and either talk over them or ignore the fact that they trying to get in – leaning forward to say something when there's a gap, getting talked over after a couple of words, then leaning back with a sigh or a slightly annoyed frown
- Is angry or upset, and starting to 'tune out' of the meeting – moving their chair back from the table, or leaning right back and glaring at the sides of someone's head, instead of watching the person talking.

You need to exercise your right to orchestrate the discussion; it's up to you to impose your presence, then say something like:

'Derek, how do you feel about that?'

'Hold on Fred, you've had a good say. Janet, you've been waiting patiently. What's your point?'

'Pat, you don't look too happy about that. Any thoughts?'

4 Watch the clock

You timed the agenda, so you know roughly where you ought to be at any given time. Many people take a lot longer than necessary to say something simple. If someone's going round the houses to get to the point, gently nudge them in the right direction. You might need to gently take over and summarise what they are saying. This stops them going on any longer and gives control of the meeting back to you, so you can decide where it goes next.

'So what you're saying is that we won't be ready until next August because of the staff situation? Lyn, what does that do to the schedule?'

But your aim is to achieve the objectives, so even if the discussion isn't essential don't curtail it if it's worthwhile. Instead, make an extra effort to keep things moving and at the end of the item take a minute to focus everyone's minds on where things are, against the planned timetable.

5 Summarise and reflect back

Summarising isn't merely useful when you want to speed up someone's contribution; it's absolutely essential, to check that everyone, you included, has heard the same things and is forming the same picture. If the item is a long one, make a point of summarising every few minutes, to confirm what you've agreed and to lead into the next stage.

'So, we've established that Jane can make it for this price, and we know there's a DIY market because Bill has done the research. Steve's going to brief the board on it and they want a test launch in the South.
We also said we need the results regularly – how do we handle that?'

Always summarise at the end of each item before moving on to the next one. It confirms the message for everyone, not least the person taking notes. To avoid any danger of confusion, make this final summary a rehearsal of the action notes and specify exactly who has agreed to do what by when. Then the notes are a confirmation of a clearly articulated agreement and not the note-taker's interpretation of what they think they heard.

6   Closing the meeting

This is easy, now you've summarised and lost AOB. It's basically a thank you for coming and taking part, and an announcement of the time and place of the next meeting.

But it's not my meeting!

When you know what makes a good chair, it's frustrating to sit through someone else's meeting when you can see they're not doing very well. You can't take the meeting over, but you can exercise some control from the sidelines without challenging the chair's authority, or implying any criticism of their competence. The question is, how?

Do:
- Make requests that steer the chair in the right direction:

  'I'd find it really helpful if we looked at the costs. Could we spend a few minutes on that, please?'

  'Would it help us to make a list of who's doing what?'

  'Could you just remind us of the timescale, please?'

- Use questions as summaries, on behalf of the rest of the meeting:

  'I am right, aren't I? We are going to do that before we do this... or have I misunderstood.'

- Prompt the chair with appropriate suggestions:

  'Last time we looked at the layout in some detail. I'd find that really useful this time, as well.'

Don't:
- Tell the chair what they ought to do:

  'We really ought to look at the costs, you know.'

- Say you know better than they do:

  'Take it from one who knows… if we don't run through that again, you're going to have all sorts of problems!'

- Do nothing: it's immoral and childish to sit there and feel self-righteous because you'd do it better, or tut-tut under your breath, or criticise the chair to the person next to you, or take some sort of perverse pleasure from seeing someone else get it wrong.

Remember, you're part of the meeting, you share the common objectives and you should want to do whatever you can to help the meeting get there.

Summary

Today we've looked at the role and skills of the chair, and some tips for staying on track, controlling the discussion and getting contributions from those with something to say. But even the best regulated meetings can suffer from awkward particpants and conflict. We look at those tomorrow and cover some extra techniques for keeping the meeting constructive when the going gets tough.

Difficult people and situations

Meetings seem to bring out the worst in some people. It isn't always easy to handle them constructively but it has to be done. Today we're building on the basic chairing skills, looking at some common problems and exploring ways of sorting them out.

Types of meeting

It's important to consider the nature of the meeting you're involved with because the dynamics change in different situations. The type of meeting has a direct effect on the techniques you can use. So are you organising:

- a team meeting, where everyone is working on the same side to achieve common objectives
- meetings of a group, either:
  - a 'political' meeting, with two sides trying to defeat each other in an argument or fighting to get the lion's share of a budget
  - a discussion forum, where people with opposing views are aiming to win over supporters.

Team meetings

Team meetings are different from all other kinds of meeting. A successful team not only works together to achieve its objectives, but also takes the time to establish how it should operate and check how well it's doing.

The secret is to make a point of taking the time to set up working conventions and develop a 'contract' for how people behave, ideally at the start of a team's life. With everyone involved, the question to discuss is: how are we going to operate so that we're a mature team?

There are several areas (there's a lot of help in *Successful Teambuilding in a Week*) to open up and talk about, so it is clear to everyone that bland meetings fail to achieve success. You need everyone to accept that the team:

- is richer when it has participants who behave differently
- benefits when people say what they really feel, even if it's a minority view or is an unpopular stance to take
- needs constructive disagreement and argument, without personal rancour or insults.

If you invest the time and trouble to build the team with care, you reap rich rewards later on. You don't need the techniques that might apply in other types of meeting because you simply don't have these particular problems.

Team roles
Not everyone has the same approach. Some people ask awkward questions; others try and build bridges when there's conflict; still others slow things down with their attention to detail. The point is that it's not only all right for different people to behave differently, it's actually extremely healthy and constructive. A sports team where everyone has the same skills and approach wouldn't get anywhere; what makes variety special is the way odd characters work together, accept each other's strengths and weaknesses, and feed off each other.

Opening the discussion up
The key is to open up the issue and get consensus to the notion that:

- each person brings different skills to the table
- each one has their own personality and style – and they'll use it because it is natural
- the team needs the full range to cover all the angles – from pushy, enthusiastic and wildly creative, to quiet, detailed and reserved.

By talking the issue through, everyone feels more comfortable about their own role. And they take someone else's different style less personally, and see it more for what it is – a natural approach and a benefit for the team.

The right to talk

Another point to set in stone from the word go is that
everyone has rights and responsibilities. Anyone with a
point to make or a question to ask has the right to make it.
In fact, it's a responsibility because the team has a right to
hear all contributions that might make a positive difference.
This isn't a problem for some people, but less confident
individuals don't want conflict, and won't risk saying
something that might make them feel unpopular or make
them look foolish. The rules here are that everyone:

- Says what's on their mind
- Listens without interrupting or rubbishing the other
  person's point
- Disagrees factually and clearly, without calling people
  names, putting them down or belittling them.

Constructive conflict

Disagreement is healthy, because it sparks new ideas and
gives a topic a good airing. But it gets personal and
destructive if someone chips in with: *'You must be kidding!'*
or *'Don't be stupid!'*

It encourages everyone to contribute when you make
rules that:

- Disagreement must never get personal
- There has to be a 'because' statement in any
  disagreement.

So instead of, *'That's nonsense!'* you get, *'I don't agree,
because…'* It also gives you the automatic right to pull
the offender up short.

Regular team 'health checks'

Once you've set the team up, make a point of checking regularly to confirm how things are going. At regular intervals take a few minutes on the team meeting agenda and pose the question: *How are we doing as a team*? Focus on the issues you sorted out at the start, and work on any points that need more clarification or discussion. And remember to celebrate when things are going well.

Other meetings

A team meeting works together for common objectives, whereas other meetings don't. They obviously have a common concern but they are coming from very different perspectives. A political meeting has opposing factions trying to defeat each other. Other meetings look at issues that concern them all, but different parties will have their own aims, priorities and often hidden agendas.

Team meetings are less likely to suffer from problems, as long as the team does its preparation properly. So what are the likely problems you'll encounter in other meetings? We looked at a few yesterday: encouraging people to contribute, stopping people who talk too much, controlling interruptions and staying on track. Other common problems are:

• Late arrivals, especially regular latecomers
• Early leavers, especially when it's a regular occurrence
• Frequent absentees
• Conflict between people at the meeting

- Aggressive individuals who bully and threaten others with their voice and their body language
- Individuals who say they wouldn't start from here, just as the discussion is winding up
- The presence of senior people and the dampening effect it can have on what people feel willing to say
- Constant jokers, who try and amuse everyone else with wisecracks and what they think are witty asides, throughout the meeting
- Those dismal people whose constant negativity can dampen everyone's enthusiasm for any new ideas and movement forward.

The 80:20 rule

There's a general rule that 80% of problems come from 20% of the possible factors. So in a meeting, 80% of your problems come from 20% of the people, while 80% of the people try hard to get it right. So if you allow the small minority to get away with bad behaviour or poor performance, it affects the innocent majority.

Always bear the majority in mind. They're completely behind you if you try to resolve problems because they don't want them any more than you do. So even if you end up upsetting the individual who isn't behaving properly, balance that against the positive reaction that you'll get from everyone else.

Regular late arrivals

This is a good example of how the 80:20 rule works.
You're running a meeting of ten people and eight or nine are
there on time. The one who isn't is always late so, knowing
they'll be along shortly, you wait for them. Stop and ask
yourself what's happening here. You are rewarding the
person who can't be bothered to get there on time and
penalising all the others who made the effort. It's simply
unfair and it gives everyone else a very poor impression of
your professionalism and chairing skills. Don't wait for late
corners. Instead:

- Start the meeting at the time you've set
- If someone comes in four minutes after you've started,
  keep going; either don't acknowledge them at all, or if
  you do, do so coolly
- Don't start again, it's their problem

- If they sit down and ask what's happened, make it clear you're not going to hold everyone else up by going over it again – be open about your position and say they'll have to pick it up from here
- Confront the issue and tackle them after the meeting – politely explain that their behaviour is disrespectful to the whole meeting, and ask them what they plan to do about it.

Early leavers

The best way to solve this problem is to stop it in advance. The guidelines we looked at on Monday covered this point; anyone planning to leave early had to give advance warning. You can't physically stop someone who gets up and starts to leave. If it's a one-off, ignore it at the time and carry on as if nothing was happening. But afterwards, tackle the person concerned and point out the guidelines, explaining that their departure disrupts attention and prevents them contributing to items that come up after they've gone.

Frequent absence

This is another problem that's best dealt with as a point of principle. It's not the most common problem but if you think it could affect you, build something into your guidelines. You should say something like: *'If you miss X meetings in a row without proper notice the meeting will automatically assume you've resigned.'*

Conflict

We've mentioned conflict in the context of team meetings, where you have more control than you do in other types of meeting. If conflict breaks out there are basically three options.

The first applies when you have a fair chance of getting things back on track swiftly, the second is for more difficult situations and the third is a last resort.

1 Look for common ground and highlight it: '*I can see there are some differences here, but you seem to agree on X, Y, Z. Let's not let this get out of hand.*'

2 Confront the situation and point out that the disagreement is becoming destructive: '*This is starting to generate more heat than light; can we please stick to the issues.*'

3 Call a time-out. Take the people concerned to one side and point out the effect of their behaviour on the meeting. You may have to come down hard, but your objective is to make them see sense and get the meeting back on track. It often helps if you get them to see how they look to the rest of the group but if they're determined to fight, invite them to leave and do it in the car park.

Aggressive behaviour

Aggressive people see everything in life as a battle, with a winner and a loser, and they're determined to beat everyone else. They simply try to impose their will at the expense of other people's feelings and views. Aggressive behaviour can show up as:

- Finger-wagging or jabbing, using it as a weapon to push home their own point and overpower someone else's
- Leaning forward and occupying the central space, pushing out everyone else and dominating the scene

- Interrupting and talking over other people
- Moving directly towards the person they're attacking, making it clear they're heading in their direction
- Talking loudly, quickly and in an agitated way, with more than enough emphasis and a tone that says they're ready to do battle
- Sarcasm, sexist and racist comments, and jokes and throw-away lines that dismiss everyone but themselves.

You won't change anyone's personality in a meeting. These people need to adapt their win/lose mentality towards win/win. But you can use some basic assertiveness techniques to influence their behaviour. These three steps are far more powerful than they look, as a way of getting positive outcomes from encounters with aggressive people, in and out of meetings.

- **Step 1**

Recognise their point of view; it shows them you were listening to them and have taken their point seriously, but it doesn't say you agree: *'I can see you feel very strongly indeed about car park allocations. They are a problem for a lot of people, when they come to work.'*

- **Step 2**

Say what you believe, or what you feel. You've acknowledged they have a point of view, and now it's time to make it clear that you have one as well, and it could be different from theirs: *'I don't disagree with your point, but we can't solve that problem here today. We're here to look at the sports day, and only the sports day.'*

- **Step 3**

Suggest an outcome that suits everyone – maybe not equally, but at least in a way that gives everyone something of a result, a win/win: *'I suggest we stick to the point about parking on sports day, and if you want to raise the wider issues after the meeting, I'll stay behind and we can talk it through. But I don't think it's appropriate for this meeting.'*

- **Repeat if necessary**

If people don't listen to you and carry on, go through the steps again. Change the words but keep exactly the same themes going. It may take a few attempts but if you hold your ground, eventually they have no option but to hear you. *'Yes, I know it's important to you. We have limited time though so we can talk afterwards, but we have to get on with the job in hand. OK?*

I wouldn't start from here…
Some people seem to enjoy throwing everything into
confusion. You've reached the end of the discussion and
they come in with a completely fresh idea – when you
asked for fresh ideas twenty minutes ago. If it has potential,
don't throw the baby out with the bathwater. It's easy to
dismiss one person's ideas, 'because it's them again'. But
sometimes they make sense and you could miss out on a
good solution if you don't think about it. It may be
inconvenient to back-track, but it is worth considering in
the light of the circumstances that apply at the time.

On the other hand, if they're being clever and bloody-
minded, you can use the same assertiveness technique
to control their contribution and move on.

Senior people
When someone more senior comes to your meeting, other
people naturally address things to them, as if they're in the
chair. Also, people often hold back in case they say
something out of line.

There are a couple of ways you can handle this:

• If they're coming for one item, put it first so you can be
  specific about when they need to arrive and when
  they can expect to leave; they're busy people so they
  will be pleased rather than annoyed
• If they need to be there for a longer period, resolve
  the problem before it arises; senior people probably
  chair more meetings than you do, and they'll have
  been in exactly this position themselves, so go and
  see them, talk through the agenda and share your
  concerns with them.

Jokers

Most people who try and make a joke of everything do so because they believe it makes them popular. But their constant search for points to joke about distracts them from playing any real part in the meeting, and also distracts the people around them. You need both immediate tactics and a long-term strategy for handling this.

Very occasionally, when someone makes a flip remark you will recognise a grain of truth in there, hidden away. If so, turn it to your advantage by saying something like *'Yes, but there's a serious point in there. It's...'* Unfortunately, more often than not, an attempt at humour is completely off the track. So, as an immediate tactic during a meeting, ignore the humour and make a relevant comment yourself, to get things back on track.

For the long term, the only way to tackle this is head-on, preferably talking to the individual concerned outside the meeting. If you put someone down during the meeting, they, and everyone else, feels embarrassed and negative. So when the time comes that you must take action, have a word with the joker and explain the effect their behaviour has on the meeting.

Explain that there are times, when their humour is really helpful, to lighten up a topic that's getting bogged down or to break the tension when there's a disagreement, and ask them to confine their comedy career to those limited times. Explain that you're having a quiet word with them rather than to point it out during the meeting, but you will have to start doing so if they keep up the witticisms.

Negative people
These people annoy everyone after a time. They're not
actively against anything specific, because they are not
putting up cogent arguments against a particular point of
view. Instead, they just moan and groan about extra work
and more cost, or say it's been tried before, or announce it
won't work here, or even just make meaningless comments
like, 'You must be joking!' During a meeting, do not let
their comments pass. You may feel that the easiest way
forward is to ignore them, but it doesn't stop them.
So challenge them to explain why they say what they do:
*'That's interesting. Exactly why do you think that wouldn't
work?'* Then try to get them to explain what would work, so
you can turn them round, from negative to neutral (if not
all the way to positive).

But it's not my meeting

Apart from the tips we covered yesterday, about chairing
from the sidelines, there's not much you can do when
problems arise in other people's meetings. The one thing
you must always do is to behave as you expect others to
behave – never be guilty of any of the crimes we've
touched on.

Summary

We've now looked at chairing a meeting, and dealing with the common problems that come with the job. We've established that teams are special meetings and that for other situations it's basically a balance: between preparation and advance planning on the one hand, and people-handling skills on the other.

HE'S JUST GETTING READY FOR THE BOARD MEETING

Following up

A regular meeting is one stage in a series of actions and progress, so it has a context. We've looked at the preparation and how to keep the meeting flowing, so as we move towards the end of the week it's time to explore what comes after the meeting. Because most meetings are in a cycle – meeting, notes, action, agenda, meeting – we can start anywhere. We'll begin by looking at the action notes that we looked at on Tuesday.

The action notes

In most cases it isn't practical to produce the final version of any minutes or notes during a busy meeting. With minutes it's impossible anyway because of their length, but with action notes you can at least check what they're going to say, before the meeting ends. One way of doing this is to use a flip chart in the meeting, as a running record and an instant reminder of the action that individuals sign up to at the time.

Individuals will generally take a quick note of their own commitments from the chart and everyone there can see what has been agreed in black and white. At the same time, you have everything you need to polish the notes and finish the job. The action notes are the trigger for action between the last meeting and the next one so they have to be watertight, without any risk of misunderstanding or confusion.

Why action notes work

The notes are not an end in themselves, they're simply a tool for triggering the action that has to take place between meetings. So the rule is: say it all, but say it in words of one syllable.

Imagine a situation where some figures are needed to put together a quotation for some new business, and the record says: *We agreed to complete the quote, once we have the materials cost.*

At the meeting a typical conversation might go something like this:

'Steve, did you get those figures about the cost of materials?'

'Well, no. But that wasn't down to me, Georgina was doing that.'

'No I wasn't. I though we said we had all we needed.'

A few more people also say it was nothing to do with them, until it's clear there are no figures and the meeting can't take the item forward. Perhaps somebody forgot to do what they'd promised, but it's more likely that everyone believes they're in the right. What's happened is that communication has broken down and everyone has their own perception of what was agreed – and everyone's perception is different.

Action notes are effective when you:

- Say enough – and just enough – to explain the key points, instead of trying to paraphrase everyone's thoughts and contributions
- State clearly every decision that was made
- Specify who has agreed to do what, by when.

This is an example of an action note that lists key points and the action people are to take. It's about a quotation for new business.

Quotation for Jackson's

1 We decided to go ahead, as long as the materials cost is less than £4,000.

2 Steve is getting the figures from production. He will circulate them to everyone no later than five days before the next meeting.

3 Everyone is to study them before the meeting.

The information is accurate, succinct, clear and unambiguous. And the note is going to be useful when it comes to putting the agenda together for the next meeting.

You could even take it a stage further and use a standard framework for action notes, along these lines.

Decision	Action	Who	By
Go ahead with quote if costs are below £4,000	Get costs from production and circulate figures to all	Steve	Five days before meeting
Discuss figures at the next meeting	Study the figures in advance	All	Before meeting

This option ensures consistency in the process at every meeting and provides a format that people get used to. The benefit of this is that when people get comfortable with a regular format, they accept it as normal and tend to become more dependable about delivering the action.

Once Steve has obtained and circulated the figures, everyone meets and joins in the discussion. As a result, the meeting is confident that they should quote, and confident they will get the business.

The overall decision to quote was made by the team as a whole. Now individual team members each take on a share of the work, to support their colleagues and deliver the quote on time. So even though the deal is not yet signed, the need to plan ahead produces more tasks for more people.

Decision	Action	Who	By
Go ahead with the quote (costs £3,870)	With all the actions below, report any problems to Jim so he can circulate everyone and 'troubleshoot'		Quote to be delivered 27 June
Inform production team	Confirm the availability of the lathes we need to produce the goods	Sam	1 June
Source raw materials	Confirm the quotes we have from our suppliers, tie them down to the price they agreed and check they have stocks available	Tina	4 June
Check we have the necessary human resources	Discuss the skills we need with Human Resource Development. Arrange for any extra training	Les	1 June
Confirm budget and payroll arrangements	Calculate overtime payments and agree them (in principle) with Payroll	Jim	4 June
Meet again to check progress and prepare draft quotation	Come ready to give a two minute talk about your progress to date	All	11 June (Agenda coming)

Preparation and distribution

There's a temptation to leave the notes for a few days, thinking you'll tackle them when you have an odd minute, but if you put it off there's a real risk that you'll forget some of the detail. That gives you and everyone else problems, so do the notes straight after the meeting. That way:

- Your memory (or that of the person taking the notes) is still fresh
- You still have a clear mental picture of what happened so you can spot any mistakes or ambiguity when you check them
- It's good time management to get an urgent job out of the way, and it's one less job to do later
- The people they go to have enough time to study them and take the action they have committed themselves to.

Use clear language

Use straightforward words and active verbs when writing action notes and avoid 'organisation-speak' at all costs. This is a common phenomenon which happens when people enter a place of work and leave normal language outside. They stop using ordinary plain words and phrases and adopt a stilted, passive and out-dated way of expressing themselves because they think it sounds like an organisation ought to sound.

So it's unfortunate, but not that unusual, to find statements like: *It was deemed to be a priority that Darren should encapsulate the detail of these points in a paper for presentation at our next meeting.* What the writer really means is simply: *Darren will prepare a detailed report for the next meeting.*

So say what you mean, and say it clearly. Use simple words and phrases and keep it as short as possible. It has more impact and it makes more sense, and everyone, including Darren, knows what they're doing.

Taking action

You've done the notes and they've gone out. You can relax – or can you? In theory it's over to the named individuals to do what they agreed to, but in practice you can trust most people to deliver their promises. But there will be a few people you know who don't always get round to things on time. If it worries you at all there's no point in standing back, wondering and worrying whether someone is really doing what they promised.

If key actions are down to someone whose time management, planning and prioritising is suspect, it can pay to check on progress between meetings, using the action notes as a checklist. If it's someone who works for you, it's a simple matter of asking them how they're getting on as part of the everyday process of management. If they're not your direct responsibility it's a bit more tricky, but there are ways that don't have to feel like a third degree interrogation. For instance, you could:

- Ring them to check they have received their copy of the notes – and while you're on the phone, ask how they're getting on with the action they're responsible for
- Find another reason for contacting them, so you have a lead-in without having to approach the question directly

- Make a point of bumping into them, and commenting how useful the meeting was and how much you all appreciate what they're doing.

Keeping in contact not only prods their conscience and memory, it can also give support to someone who is finding it difficult to make the progress they signed up for. The last thing you want is to take the job over, but you can advise, encourage and suggest ways forward if someone's stuck. It goes without saying that you need to take any action that you're signed up for, whether it's your meeting or someone else's.

Tackling tricky topics
If you had to handle a problem during the last meeting and there are any issues outstanding, such as the need to talk to someone about constant lateness or regularly leaving half-way through, do it now. Don't do it at a meeting; rather find a time when you can concentrate on the conversation, having prepared for it properly.

When you do have to address an issue with someone, always make it clear that it isn't your own personal view that concerns you. Your responsibility is to the meeting, its objectives and the people who attend, so explain to the individual why their behaviour makes things difficult. Turning up late disrupts everyone's train of thought, leaving early makes them think that this person isn't really involved, so they don't bother to keep them up to date between meetings, and so on.

Be positive and try to suggest some practical ways in which they can modify their behaviour, so you have a constructive conversation and not just a telling-off. Keeping it constructive is important, because you want to raise their involvement and commitment, and because it:

- Makes it a less stressful encounter all round
- Recognises that it's human nature to make an effort if they feel they will get some praise and respect for making a change
- Reduces the risk that they will feel under attack, and possibly counter-attack with a dogged determination to be even less co-operative
- Avoids the danger that they might comply with the 'letter of the law', but feel less involved and committed than before.

Preparing for the next meeting

We have looked at preparation on Monday, so we don't need to cover that ground again in any detail. For a meeting with the usual people, then, it's just a question of booking the room, doing the agenda and sending it out. If you have someone else coming to the meeting, make sure you brief them properly and in good time:

- Explain how the meetings are organised
- Share the format with them, and show them the action notes and agenda

- Involve them in preparing the agenda for the item they're coming for, so they know exactly what the objectives are, and roughly how long you expect it to take
- If it's appropriate and possible, give them some insight to how things might go, so they're tuned in and ready to make a real contribution.

Planning a 'health check'

We mentioned 'health checks' in relation to team meetings, but it is worth having the occasional review in any cycle of regular meetings. It gives everyone the chance to:

- Draw breath and reflect on what has happened since the last review
- Confirm where things are fine
- Look for ways of improving the meeting
- Feel a sense of shared ownership, so any success or problems are theirs as much as yours.

Simply put an item on the agenda that says 'How are we doing', to focus on what happens at the meetings and compare the way things are against the characteristics of an effective meeting that you looked at on Sunday.

Summary

The action notes are the main link between each meeting in a series. It's vital that they're accurate, clear and prompt. If you get the action notes right, you're more than halfway there. The other key points that arise between meetings are that you:

- Need to sort out problems
- Brief someone from outside who is coming to a meeting
- Monitor whether someone is taking the action they promised.

We're virtually there, now, because we've covered the main points that arise in the vast majority of meetings. Tomorrow we end with some special types of meeting that need a special look.

Special meetings, formats and problems

So far, we've concentrated on regular meetings in a cycle, with action notes and agendas to link them all together. But some meetings have a specific purpose and are different from regular meetings. For example, if someone calls a meeting for the sole purpose of giving information to a large group, it's really a presentation. Communication is basically one-way, and as everyone except the speaker is an audience rather than a participant there's a different approach from normal meetings.

But some meetings do raise some unique issues. We end the week with a look at meetings which:

- are formal, like Annual General Meetings and Extraordinary General Meetings
- are specifically set up to generate creative ideas
- have members who are in two different roles at the same time
- are called teams when they're not
- arise unexpectedly.

Annual general meetings

The AGM is a formal meeting that runs to its own strict rules. Its basic purpose is for the company board or club committee to explain the year's activities, and for the meeting to elect next year's board or committee.

How an AGM runs

The normal pattern is that it's:

- Once a year (it is an annual general meeting, after all)
- For a specified group: shareholders in a company or members of a club, for example
- Run by named officers: the chairman, secretary and the board of a company or committee in a club
- Governed by a constitution, that sets out who has the right to attend, speak or vote
- Always for the purpose of electing the officers and the board or committee
- Open to any member to raise issues that need discussion and a vote, for instance if they want to try and change policy
- Notified to all members in advance, as specified in the constitution.

What an AGM covers

The standard items of an AGM agenda include:

- Minutes of the last meeting (confirming them as a correct record)
- Matters arising from those minutes (anything that is still a live issue)
- Reports on the year's activity, from the chair and the secretary
- The financial report, which is presented, discussed and (in most cases) accepted by the meeting in a formal vote
- Election of board/committee members and any named officers such as the chair, secretary, treasurer.

Before the AGM
Each member or shareholder gets advance notice, spelling out how the meeting is to run, and the procedures for raising an issue for debate and nominating someone to stand for election to the board/committee. In most cases, issues for debate and nominations for office have to be lodged with the secretary by a set deadline, after which the secretary confirms the agenda and makes it available to anyone entitled to attend.

At the AGM
The business is conducted following the strict order and procedure laid down in the agenda and the constitution. For instance, there may have to be a certain number of people there, to make up the 'quorum' that's necessary for the meeting to take place. And the AOB slot is generally for information and questions. Unless the constitution says there's scope for an emergency resolution, an item can only normally be debated if it's notified in advance, in writing.

Anyone who tries to raise a last-minute major issue that they want the meeting to vote on could well find they're 'out of order' and fail to have it discussed.

Extraordinary general meetings

Organisations' constitutions have the procedure for an EGM written in. It's a sort of emergency meeting that takes place if a certain number of authorised people request it and sign up to a motion that they want debated and voted on. An EGM is normally to discuss a problem, like a move to get rid of the committee or the board, or a financial crisis, and it's unusual to find more than that one item on the agenda.

The formality sets the scene
With both AGMs and EGMs, the procedures and constitution spell out everything clearly. If you're involved you still need to prepare, but only for the parts of the meeting you are going to contribute to. The rest runs to its own formula.

Creative meetings

Some meetings are set up to get the creative juices flowing and to come up with innovative ideas for marketing or new products, or solutions to problems. Creativity doesn't flow best when there's a series of procedures, or a tightly planned agenda, so with creative meetings the framework is going to be much looser.

Brainstorming

One common approach to creativity in meetings started in the advertising business. Brainstorming is a process for opening up new ideas and creating a stream of possibilities, some sound and some that seem entirely wacky at first glance. But the point is that the wacky ideas sometimes have the germ of a workable idea tucked away inside them. So the aim of a brainstorming meeting is to get all the ideas out, however strange, and then look at them critically. To achieve this there are some clear rules for the brainstorming process.

1 One person leads the session
2 Their job is to:
   – explain the brainstorming process, if necessary
   – introduce the issue the meeting is looking at and start the process
   – write down every idea that comes up, without criticism, evaluation or judgement
   – make sure everyone else in the meeting also suspends judgement and makes no comment about ideas that come forward
3 The scribe introduces the issue as a question, and everyone comes up with any ideas to answer the question
4 Everyone is asked to come up with ideas – the wackier the better
5 Every idea goes on the flip chart, without criticism, evaluation, praise, judgement or any other comment
6 The scribe prompts the group when they start to dry up

7 When the flow of ideas dries up, the scribe leads a discussion to:
- group the ideas into areas with some sort of common theme
- evaluate the ideas and cross off any that are not workable
- sort the 'potentials' from the 'possibles' from the 'impossibles'
- investigate the potentials in more depth

This example has no practical value, except as a warm-up or to demonstrate the process when people haven't experienced it before. The scribe explains the process and rules, holds up a paper clip and asks: *'What uses can we think of for this?'*

The first few ideas are fairly predictable: clipping papers, a toy to play with in a boring meeting, getting a stuck diskette out of an Apple Mac computer, etc.

Then someone says, *'Make a chain and use it as jewellery.'*
Someone else starts to criticise the ideas, but the scribe stops
them and reminds them of the rules. The jewellery idea
triggers someone else to think of body piercing, so they
suggest that. Then someone else takes it a stage further and
says it could be used to perform emergency micro-surgery.
They may all sound like weird ideas, but the session is
achieving its aims: to get creativity flowing and open up
people's minds.

Wearing two hats

In some organisations, the people at a meeting are in two
conflicting roles, and this causes problems. For instance,
when a senior manager is also a director on the board, they
can find it hard to remember which hat they're wearing.
If they're there as a director, their role is to set the broad
aims and direction of the company. They set policy, make
big, company-wide decisions and have to rise above any
departmental or detailed issues. However, their
management role is to identify the strategies and tactics
to implement the board's policy, so the levels of decision-
making and debate are quite different. There's a natural
overlap in real life, but there is still a very important
distinction.

So, when a company needs to make five people redundant to save money, the board should be looking at the criteria for selecting those people so it's done fair and equitably. But when the director is also a departmental head, they can find it really difficult to put some distance between the principles and the reality. There's a natural tendency to start to look after your own, and to try and shift the problem to another department. It's not only a problem at the top level in a company; it can apply at any level, anywhere. Don't expect to overcome it entirely, but it can help to:

- Discuss exactly this issue openly in the meeting, so everyone knows that it is natural to feel this tension
- Clarify which hat people are wearing, and pin down precisely what they're here to do today, by setting the meeting's objectives that bit more tightly than usual.

Teams or groups?

This is another problem that comes from a lack of clarity about the purpose and make-up of the meeting. It's the result of the tendency to want to call anything a team, even when it isn't.

When a team is a problem

The problem could be one you've experienced, maybe with the departmental heads in an organisation you're familiar with. For example, there's a management team meeting each week, where department heads should take their lead from the board or the committee who set the policy. They should be planning the overall strategy, as one integrated organisation working to achieve its mission statement, values and corporate objectives. After all, that's what teams do – work together to achieve common aims and goals.

But in the worst cases they don't. Individuals come to the meeting determined to defend their territory or build an empire of their own, so they spend their time trying to get more of the budget than their colleagues, or to increase their influence at the expense of others. Everyone else in the organisation knows they're not a team and takes their lead from them. So each department develops a siege mentality, blames other departments and tries to score points at every opportunity.

Causes of the problem

This problem tends to be most common when there is only one round of meetings, and it's called a team. On the face of it, it's only a matter of the title but that's a very powerful tool for establishing how the meeting works and what its objectives are. We looked at teams and other groups on

Thursday so you know there are some quite marked differences between them. Because these people only meet when the title at the top of the agenda says 'Management Team', there's no other platform for arguing about the allocation of resources and other issues that inevitably need to be covered, in any organisation. So it all gets packed into the team meeting.

Solving the problem
The golden rule is: if it's a team, call it a team; if it isn't – call it something else. Think about setting up two rounds of meetings, one to do the 'teamly' things that are special to teams, and another that's called something like, 'heads of department group meeting'. That way the people may be the same at both but the context, the terms of reference and the objectives can all be set differently, so they reflect the reality of what this meeting is really for.

Unexpected meetings

We started the week by asking you to look at your regular pattern of meetings and decide whether they're worth going to. Sometimes you're asked to go to a meeting suddenly and there's no option but to go, for instance when the chief executive invites you to a meeting in half an hour. You can try assertiveness techniques to get out of it if it really does interfere with other important tasks you have to deal with, but the bottom line is that an invitation from someone senior is not normally something to decline!

For other meetings you may well have the option to decide whether to attend. The danger is that something that crops up suddenly takes you by surprise and you go along without even thinking about whether it's a good idea.

To avoid this blind rush into a meeting, apply the same critical view that you now apply to your regular ones. Don't just drop everything because someone else says it's urgent or important. Stand back and make your own judgement.

Urgent or important

There's a rule in time management, that you need to sort out the urgent tasks from the important ones. Urgent matters often aren't important at all – they just need handling quickly. If the photocopier breaks down repeatedly, it may require urgent attention because it's frustrating. But you could send the work elsewhere to be copied for now, so an immediate meeting to discuss whether to invest in a new one is probably not a priority. It's probably less important than the other things you have to do today, and that's the yardstick to use. Ask yourself: is this really urgent, and is it important? Then balance your priorities and decide whether to go to the meeting, or stay doing what you'd planned.

Important issues generally shouldn't be urgent, because you know they're coming up. For example, planning a budget is important but you shouldn't need an emergency meeting to sort it out. It should be scheduled in well ahead of time, because everyone knows it's coming round. Similarly, the need for a training course in a new skill shouldn't come as a surprise. Ask yourself: is this more important than the work I already had planned? Then balance your priorities again.

When you find that there's a meeting about something that's urgent **and** important, it's very likely to need your presence. Issues such as a threat of industrial action, a sudden price rise in raw materials when you've budgeted for orders over the coming year, or a customer going out of business overnight, are probably urgent and important. But you have to decide on the priorities, in your own context.

No time to prepare
There's little or no time for most people to prepare for a sudden meeting so there's no agenda; at best there may be a very hurried outline. But running a sudden meeting places extra pressure on the skills of the chair, because there's just as much need, if not more, for a structure for the meeting. It there's a crisis, the chair may be the only person who knows what the details are, and they have to set the scene and lead the discussion. This means that if you're in the chair, you must make time for some basic strategic preparation. In your planning think about:

- How to present the basic situation you are meeting to discuss, including what is not open to debate and what is (e.g. a customer going out of business owing you £100,000 is a fact; there's no room for discussion about how it could have been avoided – it's happened and the discussion is about what to do now)
- Whether there is a limited range of options, so you can narrow down the discussion and get the meeting to make best use of the available time by focusing on practical and relevant issues (e.g. *'As far as I can see we have only three options to look at – unless I've missed something'*)
- How to specify the outcomes you are looking for, so the meeting has clear objectives – to decide on this, or agree to that, etc.

- When there are specific issues and questions, whom you will elicit contributions from
- How to manage the meeting tightly, so it stays on track while allowing the right level of debate and discussion.

Summary

Today we've looked at some special teams, the ones that are different from the regular meetings that we've looked at for the rest of the week. Formal meetings don't pose much of a problem, because they run to set procedures and a constitution. But other meetings can be difficult, so make sure you call it what it is and spend time in the meeting clarifying the objectives, the context and the roles of the people there.

Conclusion

We started the week with a look at what makes an effective meeting, and this set the agenda for the rest of the week. It's important to get a clear picture of the sort of meeting you want to be involved with, because with a model to work to you have clearer ideas about what you need to do, and how to do it. We also discussed that:

- You should think about breaking out of meetings, and dropping them from your schedule. Do this wherever possible.
- The key to the most successful activities is the preparation, and that's where people tend to fall down. Thinking it through and getting the paperwork right gives you a plan and a framework that guides you through the meeting itself.
- Sound chairing skills are vital, as you saw when we explored the role and looked at some of the common difficult situations and individuals you might have to deal with.
- Meetings are generally only effective when they set up the essential action that comes between them, in the cycle. Using action notes and following up issues and difficulties helps keep the whole things on track.

And we ended the week with a look at those special situations that have different needs and aims. The bottom line is that the tips and techniques we covered do work, so use them whenever you get the chance or feel the need.

Enjoy your meetings!